Mrs Bobcary

Goes

John Goldsmith

Illustrated by Eleanor Newton

Pelham Books

Mrs Babcary had lived in the country all her life. Her house was a very large cello and each Spring she took all the furniture out into the garden and cleaned it and polished it.

POLISH

Of all the four seasons Mrs Babcary liked Autumn the least. For in Autumn all the swallows packed up their bags and flew off and away to the warm South. Mrs Babcary longed to go with them on their great adventure.

To the South
To the South

One Autumn day Mrs Babcary was walking in the woods, where the leaves were brown and gold above and crunchy under foot, and already there was a nip of Winter cold in the wind.

She met a strange-looking bird who wore a ten-gallon hat and had spurs on his feet.
'Where are you flying to?' Mrs Babcary asked.
'Far, far away to the great Wild West,' the bird replied.

WEST

‘It is a wild, free country,’ said the bird, ‘where the desert stretches as far as the eye can see. At night, when the moon is full, the ghosts of dead buffalo come out to play.’

Captain Babcary, a sea-faring man, was carving a new figurehead for his ship. 'My dear husband,' said Mrs Babcary, 'we must go to the Wild West at once.'

Captain Babcary did not in the least want to go. 'When will you learn, my dear,' he sighed, 'that the best place to be is at home?' But off they went in a fine paddle-steamer with three red funnels.

Captain and Mrs Babcary joined a wagon-train which wended and weaved its way over the wide prairie and Mrs Babcary said: 'Nothing at home can compare with this wild, free country!'

But then, one day, the wagon-train was attacked by a band of outlaws and bullets began whistling past Mrs Babcary's nose and she was very frightened indeed.

Captain and Mrs Babcary escaped from the outlaws and ran away into a great desert. The sun beat down on the baking sand and there was not a drop of water to drink.

'How I wish we were back by our own dear, cool, wet river,' cried Mrs Babcary.

And so, the next day, Captain Babcary found a boat with a pillowcase for a sail and they scudded over the ocean waves and up the cool, wet river, all the way home.

First published in Great Britain by
Pelham Books Ltd
44 Bedford Square
London WC1B 3DU
1980

Edited, designed and produced by
Culford Books Ltd
135 Culford Road, London N1

ISBN 0 7207 1206 8

Printed and bound in Great Britain by
Waterlow (Dunstable) Ltd.